My First Book of

How Things Are Made

My First Things

Book of How Are Made

Crayons, Jeans, Peanut Butter, Guitars, and More

by George Jones

SCHOLASTIC INC. Cartwheel ·B·O·O·K·S·®

New York Toronto London Auckland Sydney

To Tammy

Acknowledgments

My First Book of How Things Are Made was truly a collaborative effort. Many thanks to Alexandra Foley, Teri Keough, and Sarah Goodman for making the book happen. Special thanks also to the folks at Scholastic, in particular my editors Kate Waters and Jennifer Riggs, Edie Weinberg, and Angela Biola. Also, thank you Faith Hamlin, who agented the book; Megan Doyle and Tracy Hill, who assisted in a myriad of ways; and Walter Wick and Jean Marzollo, illustrator and author of *I Spy Mystery* and the other *I Spy* books for generously providing most of the wonderful pictures in the chapter on "How Books Are Made."

Also, thanks to the terrific kids who posed for me and their parents who helped out: Maggie, Catherine, and Bill Anderson; Roy, Jim, and Jacquie Dow; Max Martin, Susan Miller, and Maury Martin; Zoe, Joanne, and Ben Sargent; Ariel and Sarah Goodman; Jeremy Doo, Curtis Doo, and Susan Boehmer; Ray and Bobby MacMore, Bet MacArthur, and Bob Fillmore; Christopher, Andrea, and David Barber; Mariana, Michelle, Celia, and Michael Underwood.

The book also would have never happened without the hard work and support of the following people and their companies. Many thanks to all.

Cecil C. Barnett, Algood Food Company, Louisville, KY
Dick Boak, The Martin Guitar Company, Nazareth, PA
Jim Calhoun, Wilson Sporting Goods, Chicago, IL
James Callahan, Welch Foods, Inc., A Cooperative, Concord, MA
Brad Drexler, Binney & Smith (makers of Crayola products), Easton, PA
Michele Dryden, Levi Strauss & Co., San Francisco, CA
George Horvath, Florida Department of Citrus, Lakeland, FL
Charles Kovacs, Proctor & Schwartz, Horsham, PA
Miriam Williams, National Peanut Council, Alexandria, VA

Photographs of the children on pages 6, 12, 20, 28, 34, 42, 50, and 58 by Henry Horenstein. Crayons photos courtesy of Binney & Smith. Peanut butter: p. 12 right and p. 13 courtesy of National Peanut Council, Inc., Alexandria, VA; pp. 14, 15 bottom, and 16–19: Earl Fansler Photographers Inc., Louisville, KY; p. 15 top: Charles Kovacs/PROCTOR & SCHWARTZ. Grape jelly photos: Grafton Smith. Football photos courtesy of Wilson Sporting Goods Co. Orange juice photos courtesy of Florida Department of Citrus. Blue jeans photos courtesy of Levi Strauss & Co. Guitar photos courtesy of Martin Guitar Company. *I Spy Mystery* photos p. 58 right, p. 59 bottom, and pp. 61–63 courtesy of Walter Wick; p. 59 top courtesy of Jean Marzollo, p. 60 top: Edie Weinberg; p. 60 bottom: Color Dot Graphics, Inc.; p. 64 top: Bertelsmann Printing & Manufacturing Corporation; p. 64 bottom courtesy of Kim White, Crocodile Pie, Libertyville, IL.

LIBRARY OF CONGRESS CATALOGING-IN-PUBLICATION DATA

Jones, George, 1947–
My first book of how things are made: crayons, jeans, guitars, peanut butter, and more / by George Jones.
p. cm. — (Cartwheel learning bookshelf)
ISBN 0-590-48004-9
1. Manufactures — Juvenile literature. [1. Manufactures.]
I. Title. II. Series.

TS146.J66 1995   94-45667
670 — dc20   CIP
                                                                 AC

12 11 10 9 8 7 6 5 4 3 2 1   5 6 7 8 9/9 0/0

First Scholastic printing, November 1995

Printed in Singapore

Dear Readers,

I'll bet you've all eaten peanut butter and jelly, drawn with crayons, and drunk orange juice. You probably wear blue jeans sometimes and a lot of you may play football. Some may even play guitar. And, of course, you all read books or you wouldn't be reading this.

But where do all these things come from? They all have to be made somehow. I was lucky enough to have a chance to see how, and I want to share what I saw with you. All of the factories you will visit in this book are in the United States.

Most of these objects start with a natural process, such as oranges growing on trees or grapes on vines. But all have to be finished, usually in a factory, and sometimes the process is quite complicated. You'll see the processes unfold in this book, but I want you to pay special attention to the people who make them happen. The machines are important, but it's people who run the machines. Thanks to them we have peanut butter to eat, crayons to draw with, books to read, and all the other good things that make up our lives.

George Jones

CONTENTS

HOW **CRAYONS** ARE MADE

Crayons come in all the colors of the rainbow. With crayons you can draw a red balloon, or a shiny gold castle, or the many shades of people's skin. Back in 1903, the first boxes of crayons cost a nickel and had only eight colors: red, orange, yellow, green, blue, violet, brown, and black. Today, when you open a new box of crayons, you may have many more bright colors to choose from.

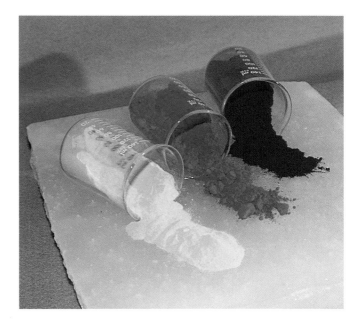

1. The two basic ingredients of crayons are paraffin wax and colored powder, called pigment. The pigments you see here are made at a color mill. First, water and chemicals are mixed in big wooden tanks to make different colors. Then the liquid flows through a machine called a filter press, which squeezes out extra water leaving a moist cake of pigment. The cakes are baked in ovens called kilns until they are hard. Finally, a pulverizer grinds these chunks into powder. The beautiful colored powders are sent to the crayon manufacturing plant.

2. Outside the plant, big storage tanks hold hot liquid wax. Each tank is 26 feet high and contains 17,000 gallons of wax. The liquid wax is pumped through large pipes into round metal containers inside the plant called mixing vats.

3. When the powdered pigment is mixed into the clear wax, it becomes colored wax. The mixture is kept at a temperature of about 240 degrees Fahrenheit — 28 degrees hotter than boiling water — so the wax will not harden.

4. This worker pours the colored wax into a flatbed mold. The mold is like a big muffin tin with many deep little holes. Each hole is the shape of a crayon.

5. Within a few minutes, the mixture in the mold becomes cool and hard. The extra layers of hard wax are scraped off the top of the mold and are melted again later to make another batch of crayons. In many factories, machines do the pouring and scraping.

6. Rods at the bottom of each hole then push the hardened crayons up and out of the mold. The freshly made crayons look like small candles.

7. One by one, the crayons are fed into a labeling machine. Each crayon is wrapped twice with a paper label that tells its color and brand name. The wrapper is glued together.

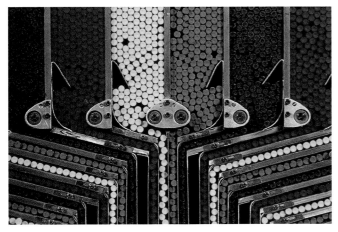

8. Then, one person checks the crayons to make sure that none of them has a broken tip. The crayons that pass the test are packed in wooden crates. Then crates of same-color crayons are moved to the packing area.

9. The crayons are put into packing machines that have different slots for different colors.

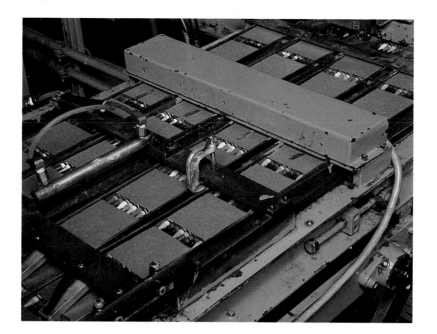

10. Here, a machine drops an assortment of different-colored crayons into narrow cardboard boxes, called sleeves.

11. When the sleeves are filled, a boxing machine puts a combination of sleeves into crayon boxes. Different machines can box different numbers of crayons. This one combines 4 different sleeves, each holding 16 crayons, to make a 64-crayon box. The crayons are now ready to be packed in cartons and shipped to stores around the world.

HOW **PEANUT BUTTER** IS MADE

Nobody knows who first invented peanut butter. People in Africa ground peanuts into stews more than 500 years ago. And the Chinese have been making creamy peanut sauces for centuries. About 100 years ago, some American doctors began recommending peanut butter as a good source of protein. Today, shelves in grocery stores are stocked with many kinds of peanut butter.

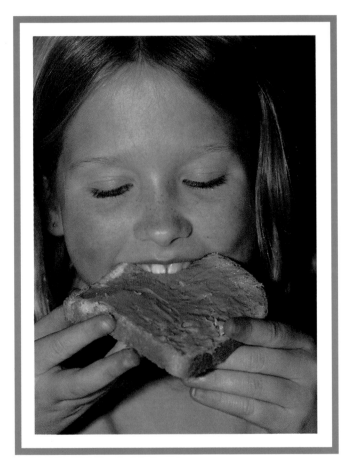

1. You probably already know that peanut butter is made from peanuts. But did you know that peanuts are really seeds? When farmers plant peanuts in the ground, they grow into leafy bushes about two feet tall. The bushes send up stalks that bend over and push back into the ground. New peanuts, covered with shells, grow under the soil at the end of the stalks.

2. In the fall, farmers drive tractors that plow the peanut plants out of the ground. The plants lie out to dry in long piles called windrows. When they are dry, a machine called a combine separates the plants from the peanuts and dumps the nuts into a trailer. Trailer trucks bring the peanuts to a shelling plant, where machines remove the peanuts from their shells.

3. The shelled peanuts then go to the peanut butter factory. First a box dumper unloads the peanuts into a gravity separator, which sorts out the heavier stones and soil that may be mixed in with the peanuts. Then a smaller machine called a de-stoner removes the last stray stones and gravel.

4. Special ovens roast the peanuts to make them taste better. Can you imagine how good they must smell?

5. After they're roasted, the peanuts go through machines called blanchers, which remove the reddish-brown skins by rubbing the peanuts between two rubber surfaces. The small gray box on top measures the color of the nuts as they come out.

6. Then the peanuts pass through another machine, called an optical sorter, which checks their color. As the peanuts travel through, any that are too dark — either because their skin is still on or because they were roasted too much — get blown out of the line with blasts of air.

7. Now the peanuts are finally ready to be ground into peanut butter. But first, some other ingredients must go into the mixers. One ingredient is sugar, or another sweetener called dextrose. The other ingredients are salt and a stabilizer, which is a vegetable oil that keeps peanut butter from separating. A computer makes sure each of the four ingredients comes out of its feeder in the right amount and gets mixed properly with the others.

8. Then the mixture goes down to the mills on the floor below. These mills grind the mixture of roasted peanuts, sweetener, stabilizer, and salt until the peanut butter is smooth and creamy.

9. Over in the laboratory, quality control technicians test the peanut butter to be sure it has the right flavor and texture.

10. Meanwhile, clean empty jars ride along a moving conveyor belt to a machine that squirts the right amount of peanut butter into each jar. The peanut butter is still warm and comes out very soft. But within 15 minutes or so the stabilizer causes the mixture to firm up as it cools. For crunchy style peanut butter, chopped peanuts are blended in as the peanut butter is put into jars.

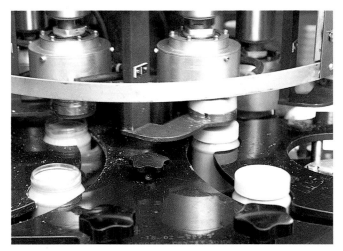

11. Then the automatic capper pops plastic caps on top of the full jars of peanut butter. The next machine sticks a label on each jar. An ink-jet printer marks it with a code that tells the jar's production line number as well as the date and hour the jar was filled.

12. An automatic packing machine lines up 12 jars in a cardboard tray for shipping. Plastic shrink wrap will go around the jars to hold them securely.

13. Now the cases of peanut butter are stacked up and ready to be sent to stores. Soon people all over will buy this nutty spread for their bread.

HOW **GRAPE JELLY** IS MADE

There has never been a team like peanut butter and jelly. They stick together through thick and thin. In fact, jelly got its name from being thick and sticky. It comes from the French word *gelée*, which means thickened. Jelly can be made out of many kinds of fruit. Grape jelly is one of the most popular jellies in the United States.

1. The dark purple color and special flavor of grape jelly come from Concord grapes, which are grown mainly in New York, Pennsylvania, Michigan, and Washington. Grapes grow in bunches on vines. Grape farms are called vineyards.

2. Grapes are harvested in the fall, when they are sweet and juicy. They are so ripe that they fall right off their stems when a machine called a harvester shakes the vines.

3. The grapes fall into long troughs on the harvester and then drop from a tube at the side of the machine into large crates. Each full crate weighs as much as two cars. Farm workers operate the harvester and make sure to stop the machine when the crate is full.

4. Truck drivers take the crates to the jelly factory. First, an inspector looks carefully at samples of the grapes to be sure they are ripe. Then a forklift operator lifts each crate of grapes from the unloading area and empties it into a long rectangular funnel called a hopper.

5. The hopper funnels the grapes into pipes that flow into a room inside the jelly factory. As the grapes are pumped through the pipes, they begin to get crushed. Then paddles push them through holes just big enough for grapes and juice to flow through. Stems and leaves are left behind. The crushed grapes flow into a big vat.

6. As the grapes are heated in the vat, they get softer — so the juice separates easily from the skins and seeds. The mixture is forced through a dejuicer or filter, which lets only the juice through. This time the skins and seeds are left behind. Then the juice is heated until it almost boils, and quickly chilled until it almost freezes. This process, called pasteurization, completely kills any germs that might have been in the juice.

7. The grape juice is kept cold in refrigerated 700,000-gallon tanks until it is time to make a batch of jelly. Then the juice is pumped from the tanks into big kettles to be cooked three times. Sugars and pectin are added to make it thicker. A worker uses a dipper to check the thickness.

8. The jelly goes into a finishing kettle for the last stage of cooking. While the jelly is still hot, it is pumped from the kettle to the filler and into jelly jars in exactly measured amounts.

9. The jars must have nothing but jelly inside of them — not even air! Germs from the air could make the jelly unsafe to eat. When a cover is put on top of each jar, the air is sucked out in a process called vacuum sealing.

10. As the jars full of jelly are carried along an assembly line, machines brush paste and wrap a label around each one. The label tells the flavor of the jelly, who made it, every ingredient in it, and the jelly's nutritional facts.

11. Before the jelly leaves the factory, workers test samples from random jars in each batch for taste and color. Machines also test samples to make sure that no air is sealed in the jars.

12. If the jelly passes all the tests, the jars are packed in cardboard boxes with sheets of cardboard between them so they won't bump and break. The boxes are loaded onto trucks and shipped to stores. The jelly is ready to meet its partner — peanut butter — on the other side of the sandwich.

HOW **FOOTBALLS** ARE MADE

You can throw a football far across a field, kick it up in the air, or bounce it in the dirt. The first official rules for the game of football, printed in 1894, said only that the ball should be made of leather and hold air. Some balls were short and stubby, while others were long and skinny. To make the game more fair, all official footballs are now the same size and shape.

1. Footballs are made from thick leather that has been softened in a process called tanning, so that it won't crack when it bends. It has also been treated with chemicals so it won't soak up water, because water could also make the leather crack. In a factory, cutters use a stamp like a cookie cutter to cut almond-shaped pieces from the leather.

2. It takes four flat pieces to make one round football with pointed ends. The ball's shape is called a prolate spheroid. The flat football pieces are called panels. Usually at least one of the panels gets stamped with a design telling the name of the factory where the football is made.

3. Next, a stitcher sews a lining that is three layers thick onto each panel for extra strength. Then, stitchers sew the panels together inside out with the seams showing. They leave a small opening in the middle with two rows of lacing holes that will be used later to close the football.

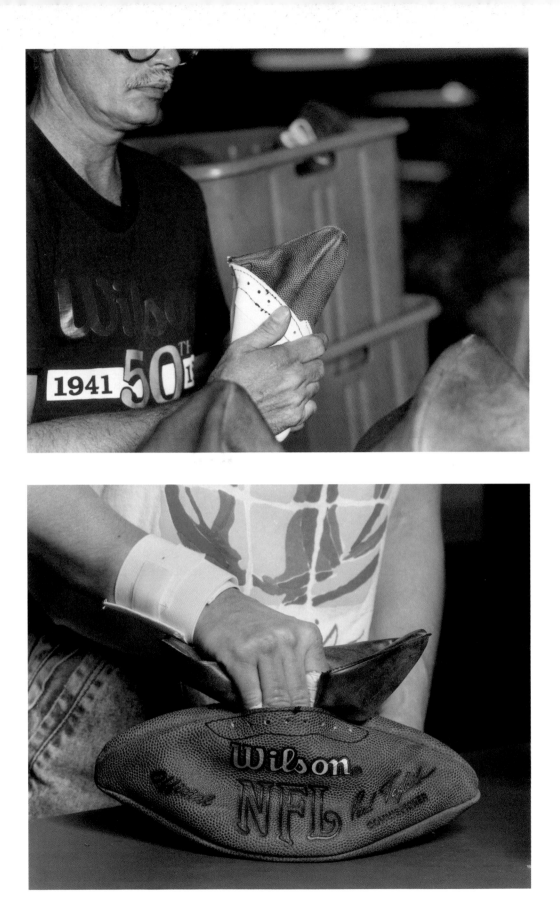

4. Turning the football right side out is no easy job. A turner has to bunch all the leather through one small hole.

5. In another part of the factory, a smaller football shape has been made from black polyurethane. This part of the football is called the bladder. The bladder is pushed in through the opening in the lace-up area. It has a valve so it can be blown up like a balloon inside the leather.

6. Before the final lacing, the football is pre-molded, which is the first try at shaping the ball. The bladder is blown up like a bicycle tire or a beach ball. This stretches the leather and the rubber and helps straighten the seams. If the seams are crooked or the leather or rubber is thin, someone will notice it in pre-molding.

7. Then the ball is deflated just a bit so it isn't being stretched. Now it is ready for its final lacing. The lacers must have strong hands. They lace the ball with strong cord as tightly as they can. Unlike most shoelaces, the cord survives rough play in water and mud without tearing.

8. A football factory can make more than one-and-a-half million footballs in a year. Every single ball must be an exact weight, shape, and lacing strength. Otherwise it just might be thrown out of the game.

HOW **ORANGE JUICE** IS MADE

The first orange seeds were brought to North America in 1513 by the Spanish explorer Ponce de Leon. Now there are more than 80 million orange trees in the state of Florida alone. About nine out of ten oranges that the trees produce will be squeezed to make orange juice.

1. Most of the oranges in the United States grow in Florida, where there are rows and rows of trees as far as the eye can see. When an orange tree is fully grown, after about 15 years, it may produce as many as 2,000 oranges in one season.

2. Oranges should not be picked before they are ready because they never get any riper once they are off the tree. When the time is right, people climb high ladders to pluck each ripe orange by hand. Pickers wear gloves and carry a canvas "picking bag" over one shoulder.

3. When the bag is full, the picker opens it from the bottom and empties the oranges into a tub. After the tub is full, a mechanical arm lifts it up and tips the oranges into a huge bin on the back of a truck. The truck then takes the oranges to the juice-processing plant where orange juice is made.

4. At the plant, drivers steer their trucks onto a ramp, which tips backward. The fruit spills out of the truck and rolls down a chute into a storage bin.

5. Inside the plant, the oranges move along a conveyor belt — like the ones at the checkout counters in grocery stores, but much longer. As the oranges go by, people check them to make sure they are ripe enough and of good quality.

6. The oranges ride along through a machine that washes and rinses them with gentle squirts of water. After the oranges are clean and have passed all their tests, they are ready to be turned into juice.

7. Extracting machines, lined up in a huge room, squeeze juice from the oranges. The juice flows through pipes to a large vat called a finisher. There, a fine screen sifts away any seeds or extra pulp (soft pieces of orange) from the liquid.

8. Then the juice goes into blending tanks. It is tested to see how much natural sugar is in the mixture. The flavor of orange juice depends on the variety of orange. If the juice in the blending tank is too sweet or not sweet enough, different batches of juice from other oranges may be added to make sure the final product always tastes the same.

9. You can find three different forms of orange juice in the grocery store: fresh, from concentrate, and frozen concentrate. The juice in a container marked "not from concentrate" has gone right from the blending tank to the bottle or carton. It may even taste something like the kind you can make yourself by squeezing the juice of a fresh orange into a cup.

10. Concentrate is a thick form of orange juice that is easier to transport and store. To make concentrate, the juice is pumped into tall evaporators, which look like shiny rockets. Inside, the juice is heated quickly to remove water until all that is left is a thick goop. A filling and closing machine cools the mixture and then seals it into cans. Finally, the cans go through a freezing tunnel.

11. A casing machine packs the frozen cans into boxes. The boxes are kept in refrigerated warehouses until they are shipped to the frozen food section of stores. People who buy frozen concentrate simply add water back into the mixture to make orange juice.

12. Sometimes concentrate travels in huge, refrigerated tanker trucks to places far away. This concentrate gets remixed with water and repackaged at its new location. Then it is sold as ready-to-drink orange juice, in cartons or bottles that are labeled "from concentrate." Even if you can't pick your own oranges, you can pick your favorite form of orange juice at the store.

HOW **BLUE JEANS** ARE MADE

When the first Levi's® jeans were made almost 150 years ago, they were brown, not blue. Levi Strauss, the man who invented these sturdy pants, called them "waist-high overalls." These first jeans were made of a heavy, canvas-like fabric. A few years later, blue denim — a material that came from Nimes, France — took its place. Today, jeans come in many different colors.

1. Most of the work of making jeans is still done by hand. The first step is to unwind rolls, called bolts, of denim fabric on a very long table. The fabric is pulled flat and smoothed out to get it ready for cutting.

2. There is a different pattern for each section of the jeans: the pockets, the waistband, and the front and back of each leg. The cutting operator carefully follows the outline of the pattern as he or she cuts through several layers of fabric at one time.

3. The front and back section of each pant leg is called a panel. After the panels have been cut out, they are stacked onto carts. Then the piles of panels are ready for the sewing operators.

4. Meanwhile, another person is sewing a design on all the back pockets. Every back pocket of Levi's® jeans has the same V-like shape sewn on it with thread. This is called a trademark design. When the design is complete, the pockets are sewn onto the jeans' back panels.

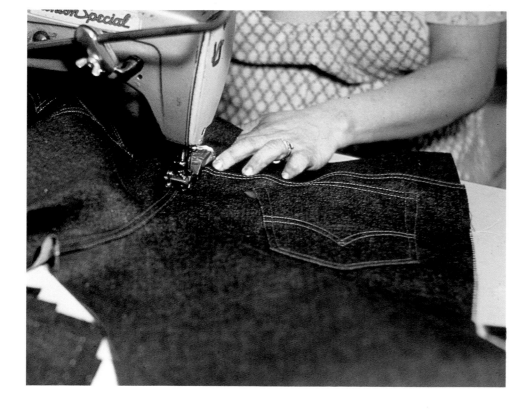

5. Then the two back panels get joined together with a seam down the middle. All this sewing is done on machines that look like the sewing machines people use in their homes, but these are stronger and faster.

6. On the other side of the room, the front panels are taking shape. These are trickier to put together. The front panels need two pockets, as well as an extra little pocket inside the right-front pocket, called a watch-pocket. Some kinds of jeans have a button-fly; some have a zipper. These, too, must be sewn on the front panel.

7. Now the finished front and back panels are ready for the main part of the assembly process. First the seams on the outside part of the legs are stitched together, then the seams on the inside of the legs. In order to be sure that the outer seams — called outseams — will stay flat, a person presses over them with a steam iron. This is called "seam busting."

8. The jeans-to-be continue along the assembly line. At each station, a person adds another piece — sewing on waistbands and belt loops and attaching buttons to the flies.

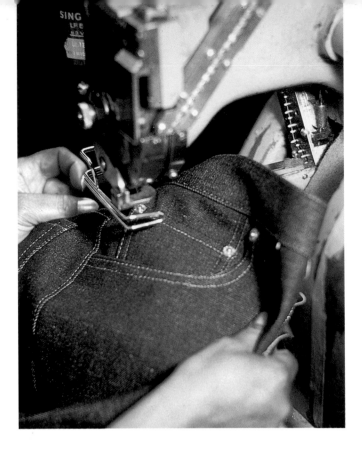

9. One of the last jobs is to tack on the rivets, which hold the denim securely in places that might otherwise rip. Each pair of jeans has six copper rivets, attached to the top corners of the three front pockets.

10. Now the finished jeans are checked by people called quality inspectors, who work under bright lights. Two inspectors look closely at each pair of jeans to make sure they are sewn correctly. While they're looking, they clip any loose threads. Jeans that are not perfect get sent back to be repaired.

11. Finally, the jeans that pass inspection are ready to be shipped to stores around the world. There they are bought by customers of every shape and size. Today, all kinds of people from cowgirls to presidents wear jeans.

HOW **GUITARS** ARE MADE

The guitar is one of the oldest and most popular instruments in the world. Distant relatives of the guitar date back to ancient Egyptian times — more than 2,000 years ago. The first instruments that looked like modern guitars were made in Spain about 500 years ago. Even today, when most things are made by machine, fine guitars are still handmade by craftspeople called luthiers.

1. The first step in making a guitar is to make the sides. This is called sidebending. The luthier selects pieces of hardwood and cuts them to size. Then he steams and bends the pieces to the correct shape with a curved machine called a bending press, which is hot like an iron.

2. The top and back of the guitar are cut out on a band saw. The top is made of a light wood, like spruce. The back is made of the same dark hardwood as the sides. The back starts out as two pieces that are glued and clamped together. An inlay strip is added for decoration. A clamp carrier can hold about 20 guitar backs flat while the glue dries. The clamp carrier travels in a circle like a Ferris wheel.

3. The color matcher makes sure the back and sides of each guitar are exactly the same shade of wood. They must also have a similar grain pattern.

4. From color matching, the guitar is sent to body assembly. The top and back must be well-braced for strength. The assembler uses braces that are made of spruce wood, like the top of the guitar, and glues and holds them in place with special jigs, or clamps.

5. After the glue dries, a scalloper uses a chisel to carve each brace with care, since the shape has an important effect on the sound of the guitar.

6. Another luthier joins together the sides, top, and back to make the body of the guitar. All parts are carefully lined up, glued, and placed in another jig, which holds the body together under pressure until the glue dries.

7. Meanwhile, the neck of the guitar is roughly cut out with a band saw. Then it is finished by hand with a variety of tools: files, carving knives, and rasps. This guitar neck is made of special mahogany wood from South America.

8. In neck assembly, a luthier cuts and glues the fingerboard onto the shaped neck. The fingerboard is made out of ebony, which is a hard, dark wood from Africa. An inlay artist insets pieces of pearl shell into the fingerboard.

9. This fingerboard has 20 frets, which are raised pieces of nickel silver. Pressing a guitar string against a fret changes the note the string makes when it is strummed or plucked. A luthier hammers each fret into a groove, then files the top of the fret smooth.

10. The next step is to trim the neck to fit with the body of the guitar. The fit must be perfect or the guitar will be difficult to play and will never sound exactly right.

11. A finisher sprays the entire body and most of the neck with many coats of lacquer for protection. (The fingerboard is oiled instead of lacquered.) All this helps protect the guitar from damage.

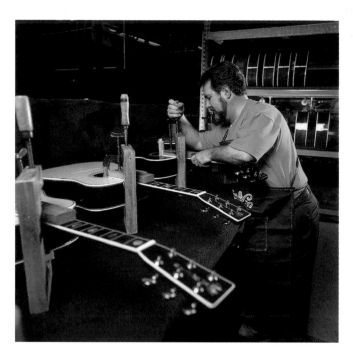

12. and **13.** At last, finishers fit and glue the completed neck and body together, using a wood-block clamp to make the bond firm. While the glue dries, the guitar rests on soft carpet to avoid scratching or other damage.

14. The finisher then polishes the neck and body for a beautiful shine.

15. The final inspector is an expert guitarist who plays the finished guitar to make sure the sound is perfect. He also carefully examines it to make sure the strings rest at the right level and that all the lacquered surfaces are smooth and properly put together. If there are any defects, he returns the guitar to the right department for fixing. Only then will it be sent to a store for someone to buy. Maybe that someone will be you.

HOW **BOOKS** ARE MADE

Have you ever made a book? If so, your book was one of a kind. All books used to be made by hand. If people wanted a copy, they had to write the words and draw the pictures all over again, every time. Then the printing press was invented more than 500 years ago. Now you see many copies of the same book in stores and libraries, and each copy is exactly the same. Those books, like this one, are made in large numbers inside a printing plant.

1. The illustrator of a book creates the pictures. The illustrator of *I Spy Mystery* is a photographer named Walter Wick. He spends days setting up complicated designs or scenes, and then he takes photographs of them.

2. The author of a book writes the words, called the text. The author of *I Spy Mystery*, Jean Marzollo, makes up rhyming riddles that tell the reader what to look for in the pictures that Walter Wick takes. She writes on her computer.

3. The author and illustrator send their text and pictures to a publishing house. There an editor reads the text, looks at the pictures, and suggests changes. The designer makes cover composites, called comps, which are suggestions for the book cover. Here the art director is showing the editors a cover comp for another book in the *I Spy* series, *I Spy Fantasy*.

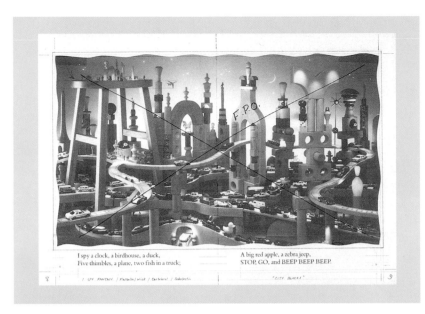

I spy a clock, a birdhouse, a duck,
Five thimbles, a plane, two fish in a truck;

A big red apple, a zebra jeep,
STOP, GO, and BEEP BEEP BEEP.

4. Then the designer lays out copies of the photographs and the text and pastes them on big pieces of illustration board, to make mechanicals. Mechanicals show where the text and photographs will go.

5. The mechanicals and the original photographs go to the color separator. There, a scanner separates the pictures into four colors: yellow, magenta (pinkish-red), cyan (bright blue), and black. These four colors can be combined in many ways to form any color in the rainbow. The scanner creates four different pieces of film — one for each color — for every page of the book. The color separator sends this film to the printing plant. The printer uses it to make the thin metal printing plates that go inside the printing press.

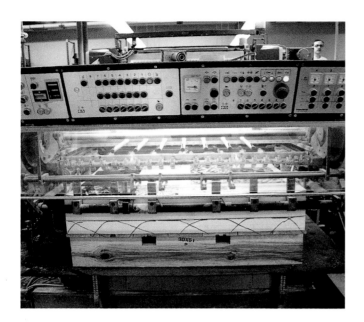

6. First the printer makes some color samples. The plates are wrapped around cylinders and locked inside the press. Then a worker sets the knobs and buttons on the control panel to print out each color. The press covers each plate with ink so it can print the words and pictures over and over again.

7. At one end of the long printing press is a viewing area. As the proofs come out of the press, the art director and the production director look at them carefully under special lights. They check to see if the colors in the proofs match the colors of the original photographs.

8. If the colors are not right, a computer can be reset to change the level of ink that goes into the top of the printer.

9. After many adjustments, it is time to print the final run. The printing press is as long as a tractor-trailer truck. The parts move so quickly that they are just a blur in this photograph. Once the press machinery gets going, it can print enough pages for about eight to ten thousand copies of the book in 24 hours. The press operates 24 hours a day.

10. Making the pages of a book takes a lot of paper. These stacks of boxes hold rolls or sheets of blank paper waiting to go through the printing press.

11. Big blank sheets that are loaded into one end of the press come out the other end with 16 book pages printed on each side. The pages are printed out of order, and some of them are upside down. But when the sheets get folded, the pages will be in the right place.

12. The next step is to send the stacks of printed sheets to the bindery. There, a machine cuts the sheets in half and folds them into sections called signatures, which in this book have 16 pages each. Another machine gathers the pages together and sews them along one edge. The other three edges are trimmed off. The long machine shown here makes the book's cover out of cloth or paper over cardboard.

13. The signatures are glued to the cover along the spine. The finished copies of *I Spy Mystery* are now ready for display in bookstores.